A Spider's Web

Written by
Michèle Dufresne

PIONEER VALLEY EDUCATIONAL PRESS, INC.

Look at the **spider** spin silk into a web.

Drip, drip, drip.
The **water** glints
on the web in the sun.

Spiders use webs to catch prey.
They make their webs from silk.

Look out, **fly**!
The silk sticks to the fly and traps it in the web.

There are tiny glue drops on the silk threads that make the spiderweb sticky.

The spider grips the fly with its legs. Yum! The spider has its **dinner**.

After an insect gets trapped in the web, some spiders will wrap it in more sticky silk.

The spider went
up the twig.
Will it slip?
No! It will not slip!

Most spiders have tiny hairs on their feet and legs that help them stick to surfaces.

Here is a spider.

It does not have a web.

It can spit!

A spitting spider spits a mixture of glue and venom onto its prey.

glossary

spider

water

fly

dinner